Every Teen Matters

How to make a difference in your Teen's life.

10 simple strategies for parents or guardians on how to help your Teen be happy, walk his GOD-given path, and THRIVE!

Written by: Delain Kemper

PRESS

ISBN 978-1-60477-979-0

www.xulonpress.com

Acknowledgements

Ⅰwould like to thank my beautiful family for all of their love, encouragement, and support while I wrote this book. I love each of you and feel so blessed to have you in my life!

To my parents: For being the best parents a daughter could have. You allowed me to follow my God-given path and encouraged me to follow my hopes and dreams. You have always given me your unconditional love and support, been there to help me through good times and bad, and welcomed me with open and loving arms. You are the kindest Christian parents a daughter could hope for. God has truly blessed me! I love you both more than words can express.

To my husband Dana: For being such a loving husband and father and for picking up the slack so I could write this book. You are such a gift from God, and I am so grateful for you every day of my life. I love you!

To my sons, Derek and Drake: For being my reason to get up each day. Thank you for your love, help and encouragement to write this book in an effort to make a positive difference. You are my precious, God-given sons, and you have made our lives so complete. I love you both around the world and back again! Watching you spread your wings and walk your God-given path is so awesome! I am so proud of you!

To my friend Daphne: Thank you for editing this booklet. I love and appreciate you!

Introduction

Teen pressure is a growing problem today, with school shootings, suicide, bullying, violence, sex, drug and alcohol abuse all skyrocketing out of control! Many of our teens are snapping right before our eyes, feeling misunderstood, stressed out, rejected and just plain unhappy. As parents, it is time to help our future adults find the balance in their lives, be understood, happy, learn to enjoy the moment, and THRIVE at being alive. We need to help them find their purpose… their God-given path, and to walk it!

God placed on my heart the need to write and share this booklet with you. I wholeheartedly believe that if you follow some of these simple suggestions, you will help your teen find harmony and joy and will have a much deeper relationship with him.

"The joy of the Lord is your strength!"
Nehemiah 8:10 NIV

Contents

1

Teen Pressure

If God has given you a teen, He has already given you the ability to help your teen through this stage of his young life. Say a prayer, take a leap of faith, and let's identify and tackle our teen-related problems together. Let's help our future adults to be happy, feel accepted, understood, loved and appreciated, and to THRIVE!

Our current teen population has been given more materially than any previous teen population in modern history, yet they are not happy. They are stressed out, misunderstood and are snapping right before our eyes! We have a generation of lost teens that desperately want and *need* to be found.

Our society today is placing tremendous pressure on our kids to be perfect, and in doing so, is giving them the unfortunate message that they are not good enough the way they are. As a result, teens are not allowed to enjoy the moment and are doggedly competing to be the best in every area of their lives.

Many are pressured to constantly prepare for their future by pursuing perfect grades, and/or excelling in sports or other activities so they can be accepted into that ideal college (preferably on scholarship), and once admitted, achieve the highest grades, and go on to obtain that perfect, highly regarded job with a six figure income to match!

With that kind of pressure, where is the time for our teens to just be kids and enjoy life? As concerned and loving parents, it is *our* job to help them balance their lives and understand that they are okay – wonderful in fact – JUST THE WAY GOD MADE THEM!

When God calls us to heaven, He isn't going to judge us by our grades, or the high schools, or Ivy League colleges we attended. He is going to be proud of those who served Him, paid it forward, and made His world a better place in which to live. With that in mind, we need to help our teens find balance in life, de-stress, work by God's speed, and simplify their lives. Ultimately, we need to give them permission to enjoy their *full* childhood before it has passed by and is too late to get back.

The kingdom of God is within you. Luke 17:21

14

2

Educational Choices

Finding the education that is right for your teen can be a challenge. Our children are living in a time when they have so many choices for their education – far more than *we* could have ever imagined growing up!

God has made your teen unique - no two are exactly alike. Each learns differently. Each has a gift at which they excel. As parents, it is vital that we take a good look at the educational paths we have chosen for our teens and find the ones that best suit them.

Since not every teen is wired to learn the same way, traditional education does not nurture or even reach all of our teens. If it did, we would not be seeing the multitude of problems in our schools. Is your teen learning? Does he like being at school? Does he feel like he belongs? Is he happy? Does he have friends? Is he going through the motions of daily school life, or is he really engaged in learning and developing himself and his talents? If you answered *no* to any of these questions, explore the different educational options available.

Your teen is not made from a cookie cutter. No *one* educational approach fits the needs of all. Sit down with your teen and really listen to his concerns about his education and school life in general. Many times, making a simple change from one school to another may be all a teen needs in order to learn and be truly happy.

Today's technological society offers many benefits, including the almost limitless educational options. Take the time to do some research, and you will be amazed by all of the choices available! Among some of the educational options to consider are:

Academic Schools
Boarding Schools
Christian Schools
Home Schools
Online Schools (public and private)
Private Schools
Schools for the Arts
Trade Schools
Traditional High Schools

There are broad educational opportunities outside the brick and mortar of our traditional educational system. *You* have the choice to educate your teen in a way that enriches his heart and soul. Go online. Ask around. Seek and you shall find! This is your teen's future. Help him to find an education that will optimize his learning preferences.

Doing so may be the *best* decision of his young life and have the most far-reaching, positive impact on everyone, including you. If your teen is not happy, the family unit is fractured, and havoc ensues.

Step outside the familiar and explore! Your teen will thank you by their favorable, self-loving actions.

Thou shall guide me with thy counsel, and afterwards receive me to glory. Psalm 73:24

3

Making Family Time
a Priority

Many of our teens are screaming for our attention and for someone to understand and listen to them.

In many homes, family time has all but gone out the window. We are so busy "doing," that even our dinners are not what they were when *we* were growing up and breaking bread as a unit. It has been proven time and again that families that eat dinner together are closer and more in tune with what is going on in the lives of each of their members. Dinner is a time for you to gather together as a family, say a prayer of gratitude to God for the day and the meal before you, and to learn what happened in your teen's life. Ask questions like, "What was the best part of your day, and why?" And, "What was the hardest part of your day, and why?" *Really* listen to him, find ways to trouble shoot, and help him through problems he may be facing. Praise him for making it through his day, and support him by letting him know you are there to help with *anything*.

Take time to be a family unit and reach out by giving of yourself - your love, a compassionate heart, reassuring hugs and smiles, and an ear to really *listen*.

> *I sought the Lord, and he heard me and delivered me from all my fears.*
> *Psalm 34.4*

One of my favorite prayers:
I surrender myself and all my problems, my loved ones, my future into the hands of God, and I trust Him.

4

Allowing Your Teen to Walk His God-given Path
(Not Yours)

Od has given each of us a path upon which to walk. He has given each of us gifts that are unique unto us.

Many teens today feel pressure to follow in their parents' footsteps. As a universal rule, most parents want their teens to have all of the opportunities they did not have growing up. This sometimes prompts them to put undue stress on their teens to do things they themselves didn't do or feel they my have missed out on, which results in a large number of teens not having the chance to seek and explore God's path for themselves.

Our children so desperately want to make us proud, and we so desperately want what is best for them! Since loving someone means having their best interest at heart, as parents, let's take the first step toward demonstrating that by allowing them to follow their *own* goals, hopes, desires and dreams. Let's be there to talk them through their options and support them in their choices. With our love and guidance, our teens will choose wisely, and we will be proud to watch them spread their wings and do what makes them fulfilled, happy and is ultimately in line with God's Will.

Each of us has a purpose; sometimes we just need a little help and patience in finding it.

Ask, and it shall be given you, seek and you will find, Knock and it shall be opened unto you. Matthew 7:7

5

Be a Mentor

Many teens today do not have a traditional family unit to help guide and mentor them on a daily basis. The challenge rests on an individual caretaker (a single mom or dad, grandmother, brother, etc.), who is entrusted with their teen's care, often due to divorce. Of course, homes in which two parents work can also pose a challenge guidance-wise, as many teens are left with too much unsupervised time that can easily lead them into trouble.

YOU can make a positive difference in the life of a teen by becoming an unofficial mentor: Welcome him into your home; invite him to stay for dinner with you and your family; take your teen friend with your family to activities in which you are all involved; get him connected with your family church and youth group (where available).

At our home, rarely is there a night when my husband and I are alone. More often than not, several teens join us for dinner. Our oldest son, Derek, is away at college, and our youngest son, Drake, is away pursuing his acting career (a younger high school graduate, he is continuing his education on-line, which has proven to be the perfect choice for him, as he is an independent learner). Despite their absence, their friends, as well as the teens they have mentored, still stop by for a hug, to have dinner, and just share time with my husband and me. We feel so fortunate – especially since we're "parents!" Through these teens, we are again surrounded by the noisy, crazy, fun house we had lost when our sons moved away - and all the joys that come from sharing time with today's precious youth.

Reach out to a teen! So many of them are simply misunderstood and do not have a traditional family unit to depend on. They so badly want to fit in, be accepted, find their purpose, and know they are okay the way God made them. It's so easy to love these kids! Just open your heart, and God will do the rest.

If God be for us, who can be against us.
Romans 8:31

6

Have Fun with Your Teen!

M any parents find it challenging to connect with their teen. It's really not that difficult if you just give it a try!

There are so many ways you can have fun together. First, find a common interest and establish a time to enjoy this activity with them on a weekly basis. Put it on your calendar, and make sure you follow through with it every week. Why not try working out together, taking a cooking class, bowling, seeing a movie your teen is interested in, even if you are not crazy about their choice, going skiing, working at a charity of your teen's choice, etc.? Or go shopping, plan a menu, cook or bake together, plan a movie night at home, play a board game, take a walk, go to a sports game, ride a bike, find a hobby... the choices are endless! It may be a struggle at first, but in time, you will *both* look forward to your shared time together. You may also want to invite one of their friends to join in or come along!

Even small or simple activities that you integrate into your typical day can help to strengthen the bond between your teen and you. My son Drake and I play a game in the car as we are driving. When we are stopped in traffic or at a red light, I get to play *my* favorite radio station. When we are moving, he gets to play *his* favorite radio station. We have a lot of fun with this, and it makes us laugh and forget the frustrations of traffic or driving in general.

Our oldest son Derek likes to take pictures and often shares them with me via e-mail or the cell phone (picture mail). We also send text messages back and forth throughout the day. (He tells me that I am getting very text savvy!) Texting is a great way to keep in touch while he is away at college - and a lot of fun. He laughs at my abbreviations because a lot of times they are inaccurate. [LOL (laughing out loud) - We send that one a lot!] Take the time to let your teen know you care and that you are thinking of him. Learn to text. If you don't know how, have him show you. Text him messages that say you love him and that you hope his day is going well.

Our kids are growing up in a completely different world technology-wise. Learn their ways to communicate, and utilize them to build a relationship that feels good. On the home front, learn what your teen is doing. I learned to play Guitar Hero and Wii with my boys and their friends, and now I actually have fun! I'm not great at this stuff, and the kids always win, but that's okay because we enjoy our time together. Just do it! Find a way to relate to them on their level.

As a family we treasure being at our rustic little cabin on the lake. There are no distractions… No electricity, no land line, and *my* favorite… no cell phone service; I love that! We are just able to enjoy being together. We love being on the water all day, and at day's end, we all look forward to making dinner and eating, talking, laughing, and just sharing time as a family. Our getaway retreat may be humble, but our family time is a little bit of heaven on earth, and I would not trade it for anything! Find a way to spend time together with no distractions. Make it fun, so everyone looks forward to doing it again and again. Find a family tradition and keep it going, no matter how busy your life gets. You will build a stronger relationship with your teen *and* have a stronger family unit.

Be in the moment. Enjoy this stage of life, because it will be gone before you know it. Embrace it before it's too late!

But as many received him, to them he gave power. John 1:12,

7

Honor Your Teen's Uniqueness

The teen years can be an awkward time. Hormonally, your teen is out of balance. Be patient with him. Try to embrace his uniqueness, and be accepting. You may be struggling with the style of his clothes or his hair, but try to remember that this stage will soon pass. If you don't react negatively, but with love and acceptance, he will likely change his style and be on to something new very soon – and probably something more favorable to you. If you react with scorn or derision, he will be more apt to keep the style going, just to get your attention or annoy you. It's just not worth arguing over these little issues. These stages pass quickly, so don't sweat the small things in life, especially things regarding your teen's self-expression.

That said, you should still offer loving guidance to your teen. He isn't perfect – none of us is… We are all works in progress, on a journey toward perfection. Rather, embrace your teen's uniqueness, and accept him through each stage. He will love you for it, and you will keep harmony in your household.

This is refreshing. Isaiah 28:12

8

Get Your Teen Connected with a Youth Group Where All Teens are Accepted

In our family, we are grateful for the blessing of having our sons involved with several outstanding youth groups. Your teen may already be involved in a youth group. If not, it would be a good idea to find one for him. Give your teen permission to try several until he finds the one that makes him feel accepted.

When I was a teen, we had religious education at our church. This program was far from being fun, and we all disliked going intensely. Find an active youth group, one that sponsors fun activities while incorporating God's Word. Youth groups can have wonderful programs for teens, including summer camp. Their summer camp programs have been life-changing for so many. (I have personally witnessed this.) If you cannot afford the cost of summer camp, most youth groups have scholarships or fundraising opportunities available.

A good youth group ministry leader can guide and mentor your teen, help him to feel and *be* understood, and gain a sense of belonging. This in turn, can help him to know God and to develop a personal relationship with Him. Your teen will come home with new friends and a new outlook on life, and you will be amazed by his happiness and hopeful attitude.

Most youth groups meet one evening a week and often have fun activities on weekends that are supervised by their youth ministry leaders. And they can always use your help. Get involved by volunteering your time. Many groups need you to open your home for supervised parties or weekly youth group meetings. They need your help setting up activities, with fundraising, or being a mentor. There are also adult prayer teams dedicated to praying for the teens and all those involved, as well as the prayer requests that come in each week from the youth group leaders and members. Yet if you can't commit your time or resources formally, simply pray on your own for the youth group your teen elects to join.

Our family is involved with Young Life, a nonprofit, national youth group (www.younglife.org). We have also been involved with Summit View, a youth group sponsored by our local community church. Our oldest son Derek is doing his internship in Youth Ministry at Pomona First Baptist Church in Pomona, California. They have a wonderful youth group! There will be similar youth groups in your area. Ask around. Call your local churches to inquire about their youth groups. The youth group your teen selects may or may not be affiliated with your church, but keep an open mind, and let him select the one that makes him feel happy, accepted, and fulfilled.

9

Families That Pray Together, Stay Together

Prayer is very powerful! Pray for your family and for our country each day.

God is with us, and he will walk with us through each challenge that we face. We just have to ask Him to be with us and to help us. Pray before each meal, and take the time to pray with your teen. Let him know that you are praying for him each day. One of the forms of prayer our family engages in is a credo we live by and a question we ask before making any decision we may regret, as represented by the acronym W.W.J.D. (What Would Jesus Do?) Use this simple prayer to call upon Jesus in your daily lives.

Another way to pray is through bible study. There are many wonderful bible studies available today. A good bible study is a terrific way to learn God's word, meet new people, and have a group that will pray for you and your family, as well as any challenges you may be facing. Seek one that you connect with.

Also, consider keeping a prayer box in your home where your teen can place prayer requests. Just knowing that someone is praying for him will make a difference in the way he feels. Remind your teen each day that God loves him and that there is no problem too big or too small for God. Our God is a loving God, and He forgives us of our mistakes - All we have to do is ask Him for forgiveness, learn from our mistakes, and make the commitment to live a Godly life.

In him we live, and move, and have our being.
Acts.17.28

10

Is your Teen Sleep Deprived?

So many of our poor teens today are sleep deprived! They are so busy with life's demands that sleep takes a back seat.

An average teenager needs 9.2 hours of sleep every night. The majority of teens get much less than that. Our body needs sleep to function optimally, and too little sleep wreaks tremendous havoc. It negatively impacts our immune system and attention span, makes us irritable and grumpy, and affects our behavior and alertness.

When your teen is having one of those terrible moods, you may want to look at how much sleep he is actually getting at night. Just because he is in his room, doesn't mean he is sleeping. A lot of teens are texting at all hours of the night, working or playing on their computers, doing homework, and are doing everything *but* sleeping! We cannot allow our teens to put sleep on the back burner for too long. Their sleep deprivation affects everyone around them.

Set some rules and establish boundaries for your teen's cell phone, computer, TV, and anything else that distracts or deters him from sleep. For example, you may want to have a storage area outside of his bedroom for his cell phone. This will allow him to sleep and not be disrupted by texts coming in at all hours of the night. Your teen will have a better attitude if he is sleeping, one that will make the whole family and everyone around him happier.

Finally, give your teen permission to sleep-in one day a week (Saturday or Sunday if he is in a traditional school). Your teen will thank you by his good mood. He will get more accomplished when he is awake since his body will be fully recharged, thereby enabling him to tackle his schedule much more easily and effectively.

A message from the author:

As a parent, it is your responsibility to take the time to tell your teen you love him (often and much), to enjoy the moment, and to enjoy this day. It's all we have! There are no guarantees. Embrace this day – today – and every day with your teen. Tell him how very special he is and how proud you are of him! Give him lots of hugs each day. Be there for him. Simply take the time to tell your beloved teen that you care and are proud to be his parent! Pray for him, and remind him over and over of how very much God loves him and you love him.

Together, we can make a difference, one teen at a time.

In his light and love,
Delain

Suggested readings:

My favorite booklet that our family loves to share with others is *Thought Conditioners* by Norman Vincent Peale. To order, call Guide Posts at 1-800-936-0158, ext. 43. There is a $1.00 donation for each booklet. You may want to order more of them and give them away. You will be glad you did. This booklet will make a difference in your life and in the lives of others.

Dr. James Dobson has many great books available at most book stores that deal with raising kids. (My favorite is *Bringing up Boys*.)

Another excellent source of help and information is the Karen Kingsbury collection. Her books are very uplifting and are available at most bookstores.